Foreign Relations
of the
United States
Diplomatic Papers
1940
(In Five Volumes)

Volume III
The British Commonwealth
The Soviet Union
The Near East and Africa

United States
Government Printing Office
Washington : 1958

DEPARTMENT OF STATE PUBLICATION 6638

———

For sale by the
Superintendent of Documents, U.S. Government Printing Office
Washington 25, D.C. - Price $4.50 (Buckram)

CONTENTS

THE BRITISH COMMONWEALTH OF NATIONS

UNITED KINGDOM

RESPONSE OF THE UNITED STATES TO APPEALS FOR GREATER ASSISTANCE TO THE BRITISH WAR EFFORT[1]

841.24/263

Memorandum by the Chief of the Division of Controls (Green)

[WASHINGTON,] March 18, 1940.

I called this morning by appointment on Captain Collins, Chief of the Procurement Division of the Treasury and Chairman of the Interdepartmental Liaison Committee established by the President to deal with foreign purchasing missions. I explained that I had asked for an appointment in order to ascertain from him just what he wished the Department of State to do in connection with the work of his Committee. I pointed out that correspondence between his office and the Department in regard to this matter had followed no regular pattern and suggested that the establishment of some definite procedure agreeable to him might be advantageous.

Captain Collins readily agreed. He said that the whole machinery of the Liaison Committee was new; that the Committee had been almost swamped by the pressure of business; and that contacts with the Department of State had heretofore been rather haphazard. He said that he welcomed my call as a means of establishing proper and definite liaison with the Department of State.

After some discussion, it was agreed that representatives of foreign governments, whether diplomatic representatives or agents specifically charged with making purchases, who might call at the Department with a view to making arrangements for the purchase of munitions, were to be referred to him, except when the proposed purchases were to be purchases of arms declared surplus by the War Department. In each case, when the representative of a foreign government was referred to his office, he would be notified by a third person letter. Representatives of foreign governments referred to Captain Collins would be informed by the Department that they could carry on all negotiations directly with him and that it would not

---

[1] For correspondence with regard to establishment of an Anglo-French Purchasing Board for coordinating British and French purchasing in the United States, see *Foreign Relations*, 1939, vol. I, pp. 562 ff.

be necessary to transmit requests for information or for action through the Department of State. The Department would in all cases be informed in writing of the decisions of the Committee—for information only in case the purchasing agent is not the diplomatic mission of the purchasing government accredited to this Government, and for transmission to the appropriate embassy or legation in case the purchasing agent is a diplomatic officer accredited to this Government. In the latter case, the decisions would be transmitted in duplicate, the papers drafted in such wise that copies could be forwarded to the appropriate mission.

Captain Collins agreed that requests to negotiate for the purchase of surplus arms should not be referred to his Committee but should be referred directly to the War Department in accordance with the procedure already agreed upon between the Secretaries of State and War.

Joseph C. Green

740.00111A Armed Merchantmen/39

Memorandum of Telephone Conversations, by the Assistant Chief of the Division of European Affairs (Hickerson)

[Washington,] May 14, 1940.

Mr. Hoyer Millar [2] telephoned me yesterday afternoon and stated that the British Embassy had just received a telephone call from Sir Ashley Sparks, the New York representative of the British Ministry of Shipping, who stated that he had learned that there might be difficulty in connection with clearing British merchant vessels which entered American ports with defensive guns installed and, while in American ports, had degaussing equipment (to neutralize magnetic mines) installed. Mr. Hoyer Millar inquired whether there was any information which I could give him on this subject. I replied that I understood that the question was under consideration, and that I would be glad to let him know when a decision on the point had been reached.

This morning Mr. Hoyer Millar telephoned again, and said that he had had another telephone call from Sir Ashley Sparks, with particular reference to the British merchant vessel *Brittanic*, which is now in New York, which entered the port as an armed merchant vessel and on which the British Government desires to have degaussing equipment installed in New York. He said that Sir Ashley Sparks had gathered from inquiries in New York that there would be no difficulty about clearance for an unarmed merchant vessel which had degaussing equipment installed in an American port, but that they

---

[2] First Secretary of the British Embassy.

were particularly anxious to have such protective equipment placed on the *Britannic* and other British merchant vessels. He added that he would be appreciative if I would call him just as soon as possible when there was information available.

Immediately after the Secretary signed a letter of today's date on this subject to the Secretary of the Treasury,[2a] Mr. Carlton Savage [3] was good enough to bring it to me on his way to the Treasury Department to deliver the letter. I told Mr. Savage that I would wait until mid-afternoon before telephoning Mr. Hoyer Millar in order that the Treasury and Commerce Departments might have time to issue their instructions on the subject. At 3 : 30 this afternoon I called Mr. Hoyer Millar and told him that it had been decided that degaussing equipment could be installed on merchant vessels, armed or unarmed, in American ports. He expressed his appreciation.

J[OHN] D. H[ICKERSON]

841.24/260½

Memorandum of Conversation, by the Under Secretary of State
(Welles)

[WASHINGTON,] May 23, 1940.

The British Ambassador [3a] called to see me this evening at his request. The Ambassador went over the main points in a conversation which Mr. Purvis, British member of the Allied Purchasing Mission in the United States, had had the preceding evening with the Secretary of the Treasury and high officials of the War and Navy Departments. The Ambassador stressed the importance of the requests which the British Government had made for the sale to it by the United States of airplanes and various categories of armament and ammunition. I told the Ambassador that, by instruction of the President, General Marshall [4] had visited me in the morning and had shown me a tentative list which he had prepared indicating the amounts of artillery and ammunition which the War Department could sell to the British Government by declaring these stocks surplus and as not being required for the national defense of the United States. I said that it was my understanding that the list so formulated was as yet tentative and that it would later be supplemented by a definitive list. I further said that it was my understanding that some of the categories could be transferred to private manufacturers in the United States under existing law in return for new stocks of the same types. In such

---

[2a] Not printed.
[3] Assistant to the Counselor of the Department of State.
[3a] Marquess of Lothian.
[4] Gen. George C. Marshall, Chief of Staff, United States Army.

cases, I said, I had been given to understand that the private manufacturers could then sell directly to the British Government, and there
would consequently be involved no breach of the neutrality of the
United States under international law and no breach of the existing
neutrality act.[5] With regard to other categories on the list, I said
I had been informed that no such transfers to private manufacturers
could be undertaken, and that the question therefore was one of the
highest policy which of course could be determined only by the President in consultation with the highest appropriate members of the
Administration.

The Ambassador said that he understood this situation fully, but
that he earnestly hoped that a speedy decision could be reached. He
said it was of vital importance to Great Britain to obtain these supplies within the shortest period humanly possible.

The Ambassador inquired whether I had any recent information
from Italy, and I told him that the information which the Department
had received continued to show that Italy was making preparations
to enter the war but as yet there was no positive indication as to when
that move would take place.[6]

The Ambassador then discussed, as he had done before, the possi-
bilities inherent in the present situation and the attitude which the
British Government would take in the event that Germany succeeded
in defeating France and then either succeeded in invading England
and forcing submission or undertook an intensive bombing campaign
of England with great resultant destruction of life and property. The
Ambassador in very vigorous terms stated that it was his positive conviction that so long as the British and French fleets remained intact
and out of German hands and so long as the United States fleet
remained in the Pacific, and the Allied fleets therefore controlled the
Atlantic and the United States was able to act as a counterpoise to
Japan in the Pacific, Germany could not eventually win the war. He
said in this connection that he believed it was of imperative importance
that the American fleet at this time should remain in the mid-Pacific
since that was the only effective check on Japan which existed in the
world today. He said he was further confident that no British Government would surrender the fleet, and that the high ranking naval
officers in command of the fleet would never agree to surrender the
fleet even if ordered to do so. He said he was positive that even if
a majority of the House of Commons voted in a new government
which would agree to surrender the fleet, the present British Government would refuse to acquiesce in any such decision and would remove
to Canada, where the British fleet could at least in part be based, other

[5] Neutrality Act of 1939 ; 54 Stat. 4.
[6] For correspondence on efforts of the United States to keep Italy from entering
the war against the Allies, see vol. II, pp. 685 ff.

portions of the fleet being based on the British West Indies or perhaps off South Africa. I gained the very definite impression from the positive terms in which the Ambassador spoke that he had received some communication upon this subject recently from Mr. Churchill [7]— presumably after the Ambassador's last conference with the President.[8]

S[UMNER] W[ELLES]

841.248/449

The Prime Minister of Australia (Menzies) to President Roosevelt [9]

In this hour of great emergency not only for Great Britain and France but also for Australia and the other British Dominions, I desire to put before you certain considerations.

Though we are determined to win and are by no means anticipating defeat, it is still obviously possible that France may be defeated and that in such an event Great Britain's power to resist Germany will depend on her navy and her ability to resist or prevent an attack.

This would mean that air strength would become vital and I do not need to point out to you that Germany has great numerical preponderance. Successful attacks upon factories interrupting production might be decisive.

I hope that you will not find me unduly unconventional if I say to you as the head of the greatest but most friendly neutral power that to prevent the British fleet falling into German hands must be of the greatest importance to the U. S. A. and that I cannot believe the U. S. A. can view with anything but acute anxiety a Europe completely dominated by Germany and a victorious Germany exercising undisputed power in the Eastern Atlantic and adjoining seas. One must also remember that in the event of a defeat to Great Britain the possession of West Indian islands would undoubtedly be demanded by Germany.

I believe that your great country has it in its power to make a decisive contribution without actually participating. The one country that can rapidly and substantially increase British air power is U. S. A. and even if this means despatch to Great Britain of machines already in commission in or designed for your own Air Force, I would most earnestly urge you to follow that course.

I am quite confident of British capacity to meet all attacks against the United Kingdom and in turn to inflict such damage upon Germany as to produce her defeat—provided the United States can supply the additional aeroplanes which are needed. But quite plainly—

---

[7] Winston Churchill, British Prime Minister.

[8] For correspondence with regard to concern of the United States over the fate of the British Fleet, see pp. 29 ff.

[9] Transmitted by the Counselor of the Australian Legation, Keith Officer, to the President on May 26, 1940; copy left at the Department by Mr. Officer on the same date.

and I know that you would wish me to speak plainly—without most prompt assistance from the United States there must be a grave danger of a state of affairs developing, more or less quickly, in which the power of Great Britain to defend liberty and free institutions is destroyed and in which we, your English-speaking neighbours across the Pacific basin, must find our own independence, it seems, imperilled.

There is in Australia a great belief in your friendliness and good-will. We feel that we are fighting for immortal things which you value as we do and on behalf of my own people I beg for your earnest consideration and swift action.

811.22742/310

Memorandum of Conversation, by the Under Secretary of State
(Welles)

[WASHINGTON,] May 27, 1940.

The British Ambassador called to see me this morning with the Canadian Chargé d'Affaires, Mr. Mahoney. The Ambassador stated that the British and Canadian Governments desired to ascertain whether the United States Government would permit or possibly facilitate the training of British and Canadian pilots in governmental schools and airfields. The Ambassador stated that such pilots would come to the United States in a civilian capacity and as individuals.

The Ambassador stated that he understood that I had been informed of this matter beforehand.

I said to the Ambassador that, as Mr. Mahoney knew, the views of this Government had been communicated some days before to the Canadian Prime Minister with reference to the enlistment of American citizens in Canada for service in the British and Canadian air forces, but that I had had no prior knowledge of the request the Ambassador had just made of me except a cryptic message [10] from Ambassador Kennedy [11] saying that Lord Lothian would discuss with me an aviation question and that the Ambassador felt it would be better to handle the matter in Washington rather than in London.

I stated to Lord Lothian and to Mr. Mahoney that it seemed to me there were two questions involved, first, whether the proposed step would violate any of our neutrality requirements, and, second, whether the facilities now existing in the United States would be sufficient to make possible the training of non-American pilots other than the few which we took from the other American Republics. I said this latter problem seemed to me difficult to overcome in view of the present rearmament program and in view of the fact that Lord Lothian had indicated that something like one hundred thousand aspirants had

[10] Not printed.
[11] American Ambassador in the United Kingdom.

registered for training as pilots in Canada and in Great Britain. In order to answer these two questions, I said I would have to consult certain of the appropriate authorities of this Government and I said that I would inform the Ambassador of our decision as soon as might be possible.

S[UMNER] W[ELLES]

841.248/452

The Under Secretary of State (Welles) to the Australian Minister (Casey)

WASHINGTON, June 1, 1940.

MY DEAR MR. MINISTER: I immediately transmitted to the President the personal and confidential message from Mr. Menzies which was left at the Department by Mr. Keith Officer on May 26, 1940. The President has asked me to send to you for transmission to Mr. Menzies his personal and confidential reply to that message. The President's reply [12] is quoted below.

"I was glad to receive on May 26th your personal message, which I have read with interest and considered with care.

"I fully realize that the Allies are facing a critical situation in Europe, and I of course understand and appreciate the motives which prompted you to send me this message. I do not think that there are many people in the United States, and certainly none in the Executive Branch of our Government, who fail to appreciate the implications and dangers to the whole world of the triumph of those forces against which your country is struggling, and I want you to know that, subject to the necessary limitations of the position of this country, the production facilities of the United States are available in their entirety to the Allies.

"With regard to your specific suggestion concerning the need of planes by the Allied Governments, I may say that a large number of planes have been ordered in this country by those Governments, and sizable quantities have already been delivered. We do not expect that the armaments program of the United States will interfere in any way with the speedy delivery of planes for the Allied Governments. When I sent a message to Congress on May 16th dealing with the necessity for increasing the armaments of the United States, you may have noted that I made the following statement:

" 'For the permanent record, I ask the Congress not to take any action which would in any way hamper or delay the delivery of American-made planes to foreign nations which have ordered them, or seek to purchase more planes. That, from the point of view of our own national defense, would be extremely shortsighted.'

"I deeply appreciate and cordially reciprocate your friendly references to me and to the United States."

Believe me [etc.]   SUMNER WELLES

---

[12] President Roosevelt addressed a similar message to the Prime Minister of New Zealand in reply to the latter's appeal for aid for the United Kingdom.

811.22742/310

Memorandum of Conversation, by the Chief of the Division of European Affairs (Moffat)

[WASHINGTON,] June 4, 1940.

At Mr. Welles's request, I asked Mr. Merchant Mahoney, the Canadian Chargé d'Affaires, to call in order to discuss with him the question of facilitating the training of Canadian pilots in American Governmental schools and airfields which Mr. Mahoney had raised with the Under Secretary on May 27.

I told Mr. Mahoney that the problem had been considered very carefully and sympathetically by the Secretary of State, the Under Secretary, the Chief of Staff, and others. The conclusions reached were that the apprehensions felt by Mr. Welles in his talk of May 27 were well founded. These apprehensions rested on two grounds, a practical one and a legal one.

As a practical matter, a project of training Canadian pilots in this country on a large scale obviously could not be carried on concurrently with a similar training program for our own air corps which contemplates using Army and Navy civilian facilities and personnel to the maximum. Apparently, the bottleneck is flying instructors and, to a lesser degree, training planes. Already in order to turn out the number of pilots we consider essential in 1941 and 1942 we are using as instructors all Army instructors, all qualified officers now in the Training Center and civilian schools, all qualified officers who could be made available by the suspension of miscellaneous activities, qualified civilian instructors, et cetera. Thus, any large-scale plan of training Canadian pilots would retard the work being done for us at the Training Centers, and the lack of additional flying instructors prevents the use of other military flying fields for training schools.

With regard to legal considerations, the legal advisers of the competent Government departments have held that if the pilots were members of the Canadian military or naval forces they could not be trained in this country without a violation of The Hague Convention No. V,[13] nor, in their opinion, could such training be legalized short of amendment or denunciation of this international treaty. This, of course, would not apply to Canadian civilians, particularly if they came to this country for training without advance arrangement between Governments calling for such admissions in specific numbers or groups with a definite view of their later employment in a belligerent army; but the Chief of Staff has added that even these civilians could not be accepted as students at the Air Corps Training

---

[13] Foreign Relations, 1907, pt. 2, p. 1216.

Centers without additional statutory authority (see Act of April 3, 1939 [14]).

The conclusion reached by our military authorities, in which other Government officials concurred, was that irrespective of legal restrictions, the diversion of any considerable pilot production to the training of Canadian pilots would disrupt our own training program and would seriously delay bringing our own air defenses into a satisfactory state of readiness. It was therefore hoped that the Canadian authorities would choose not to press this particular request.

Mr. Mahoney stated that there seemed to be a slight difference of emphasis between the Canadian request and our reply. The Canadian request merely referred to "a number of aviators" to be trained, whereas our reply was based on a large-scale training project which he personally doubted was the case. The other shift in emphasis was that whereas the Canadian request had referred to "civilian training schools", our reply referred to Army Training Centers. I told Mr. Mahoney that as I understood matters, the Training Centers were taking over all instructors and that there would be no civilian schools in the future.

Mr. Mahoney said that he would bring the information at once to the attention of Ottawa.

P[IERREPONT] M[OFFAT]

811.22742/310

Memorandum of Conversation, by the Under Secretary of State (Welles)

[WASHINGTON,] June 5, 1940.

The British Ambassador called to see me this morning at my request.

With regard to the Ambassador's request made on May 27, namely, that British and Canadian pilots be trained in American aviation training centers, I said that the matter had been given very full consideration and that without reference to legal considerations, the practical situation was that we were now planning in our own rearmament program to use army and navy as well as civilian facilities and personnel to the maximum, and our military and naval authorities did not believe that it would be possible, at least for some time to come, to consider the training of any foreigners other than those already in service schools.

The Ambassador said he had anticipated this reply but wondered if there was not something outside of this particular aspect which could be done. He asked whether it would not be possible for this

---

[14] 53 Stat. 555.

Government to permit the British and the Canadians to rent and utilize air fields in the southern states during the coming autumn and winter when Canadian fields would be out of commission because of the Canadian winter weather.

I told the Ambassador that I would be very glad to study this question and to let him know what the authorities here thought could be done in this regard.

S[UMNER] W[ELLES]

740.0011 European War 1939/3870

Memorandum of Conversation, by the Secretary of State

[WASHINGTON,] June 6, 1940.

The Australian Minister [15] called at his request. He took as his text the joint view of himself and Minister Bruce, now representing Australia in London, to the effect that Germany could, in their judgment, capture Great Britain. He was very emphatic in expressing this view. The Minister indicated that since this country was doing about all it could in every legitimate and practical way to sell equipment and supplies to the Allied belligerents, he would be extremely interested to see this Government make a declaration of war. I promptly said to him that this was unthinkable in the present situation. I then reviewed just what was being done. He stated that the moral effect of a declaration of war by the United States would be very great. I again summarily dismissed this idea and reminded him that this country was doing all possible in the circumstances, as stated, without becoming involved in a military war or making a military alliance. This was about the burden of the conversation.

C[ORDELL] H[ULL]

841.248/469¼ : Telegram

The Ambassador in the United Kingdom (Kennedy) to the Secretary of State

LONDON, June 6, 1940—2 p. m.
[Received June 6—8:30 a. m.]

1522. Personal for the President and the Secretary. Following letter dated June 5 received from Beaverbrook: [16]

"I shall be glad if you will transmit the following message to the President of the United States.

Beaverbrook has received message through Lothian and Halifax [17]

---

[15] Richard G. Casey.
[16] Lord Beaverbrook, British Minister for Aircraft Production.
[17] Lord Halifax, British Secretary of State for Foreign Affairs.

that you have offered to permit us to buy civil aircraft for short range night bombing of the following types: Lockheeds 12 and 14, Beechcraft, Cessna, Spartan, and others.

Beaverbrook is most grateful to the President for this suggestion. He has already applied for three Lockheeds and he hopes to take more for troop carrying. But the other types are not suitable for us because we are short of equipment, and have no material for armoring and arming, apart from supplies already needed for aircraft in storage here. What we need are operational types with equipment and armament and ammunition. And anything done for us would be a little bit of heaven. Signed Beaverbrook."

KENNEDY

811.22742/310½

The British Ambassador (Lothian) to the Under Secretary of State (Welles)

WASHINGTON, June 8, 1940.

DEAR MR. UNDER SECRETARY: With reference to our conversation on June 5th regarding the possibility of training British air pupils in this country, may I set forth in a little more detail the alternative suggestion I made about facilities for training British or Canadian pilots in the United States of America. It would be of very great assistance to my Government if it were possible for two or three landing grounds suitable for use all the year round to be placed at our disposal where the flying training of pupils could be carried out on civilian aircraft and with civilian instructors. The pupils themselves would also be civilians and the training would be carried out under civilian conditions. The direction and control of the schools themselves might well be under the auspices of United States personnel. If such facilities could be granted they would be of the greatest value, more especially in the spring and autumn when flying training in Canada presents obvious difficulties.

LOTHIAN

841.248/452

The Prime Minister of Australia (Menzies) to President Roosevelt [18]

MR. PRESIDENT: I recently had the honour to communicate with you on the subject of possible United States assistance to the Allied arms. Since then the position has become rapidly grave and as it might well become worse, I do not exaggerate when I say that as a British and democratic country we are forced to contemplate the possibility of a beaten France and a Great Britain in danger of being overwhelmed

---

[18] File copy on letterhead of the Australian Legation, not signed.

not by superior courage or by a good cause but by a villainous com-
bination of international lawlessness and a long-prepared mechanism
of superiority.

In certain events we in Australia may have to fight for our own
lives and I want to tell you that with all the defects of our equipment
we will fight for them to the end.

At this moment the eyes of the whole liberty-loving world are turned
to you and your great people.

I believe even now, if the United States, by a magnificent and
immortal gesture, could make available to the Allies the whole of their
financial and material resources, Germany could be defeated. The
effect on the spirit of France would be transfiguring while the whole
of the English-speaking peoples of the world would by one stroke be
welded into a brotherhood of world salvation.

On behalf of the people of Australia and the future of this land I
appeal to you for the fullest possible measure of co-operation and help.

14 JUNE, 1940.

841.248/498

The Under Secretary of State (Welles) to the Australian Minister (Casey)

WASHINGTON, June 20, 1940.

MY DEAR MR. MINISTER: The President has asked me to send to you
for transmission to Mr. Menzies his reply to Mr. Menzies' personal
message of June 14. The President's reply is quoted below:

"Mr. Prime Minister: I acknowledge with appreciation your further
personal message on the subject of possible United States assistance
to the Allied Governments. I have given your message my most
earnest and most friendly consideration.

"I am fully aware that the Allies are facing a critical situation, the
gravity of which has even increased since the receipt of your message,
and I do not fail to appreciate the dangers to the United States and to
the world implicit in an Allied defeat. For these reasons I have
repeatedly made clear to all the world that the whole of American sym-
pathies lies with the Allied Governments. In my speech of June 10 [19]
I announced the intention of the United States Government to extend
to the Allies the material resources of the nation. Pursuing that policy
with every effort, this Government has made it possible for the Allies
to obtain in this country quantities of arms and munitions and
airplanes.

"In my message to the Premier of France on June 15 I stated:

" 'In these hours which are so heart-rending for the French people and yourself,
I send you the assurances of my utmost sympathy and I can further assure you

---

[19] At the University of Virginia; for text of speech, see Department of State
Bulletin, June 15, 1940, p. 635.

that so long as the French people continue in defense of their liberty which constitutes the cause of popular institutions throughout the world, so long will they rest assured that matériel and supplies will be sent to them from the United States in ever-increasing quantities and kinds.

" 'I know that you will understand that these statements carry with them no implication of military commitments. Only the Congress can make such commitments.'

"In a like manner and subject to the same limitations I want to assure you that so long as the peoples of the British Commonwealth of Nations continue in the defense of their liberty, so long may they be assured that matériel and supplies will be sent to them from the United States in ever-increasing quantities and kinds.

"Franklin D. Roosevelt."

I am [etc.] SUMNER WELLES

711.42/193 : Telegram

The Minister in Canada (Moffat [20]) to the Secretary of State

OTTAWA, June 23, 1940—7 p. m.
[Received 10 : 25 p. m.]

147. For the Secretary and Under Secretary. The following summary of the situation in Canada, although necessarily based on first impressions only, may prove useful by way of background.

1. Canada to date has had few if any war plans of her own. She has done exactly what the British Government asked and the British requests were based on the premise that the Maginot Line would hold and enable the Allies slowly but relentlessly to build up their armies and their reserves of equipment. Even the Empire air training scheme was predicated on Great Britain's supplying most of the training planes, it was to proceed at a leisurely pace with the first classes of trained aviators being used as instructors for subsequent classes, et cetera. In the general matter of equipment the British have insisted on the standardization of parts so that British and Canadian equipment would be interchangeable. This would not have been so unfortunate if the British had decided early in the war on certain basic types of tanks, engines and other material and promptly supplied drawings: but one hears of so many instances where drawings were withheld, plans changed after tooling has begun, orders canceled in the interest of economy.

2. With Allied reverses, all this has changed.

3. The first effect of the reverses was to disrupt the Empire air training scheme. The British informed the Canadians one day that the promised training planes could not be delivered, they recalled almost all their inspectors and they asked that every available Canadian aviator be sent to England the moment his training was finished.

---

[20] Jay Pierrepont Moffat was assigned to the post June 4, 1940.

Now the Canadians are scouring the United States for planes, engines, equipment and even instructors to salvage as much as possible of the scheme.

4. The second effect was a realization from one end of the Dominion to the other that this leisurely pace must give way to a maximum effort. That is the real meaning of Mackenzie King's [21] "war mobilization bill" which is supported by heavy majorities even in Quebec. Except for conscription for overseas service, against which there is still a strong sentiment in many quarters. All of Canada is asking for the chance to contribute as fully as possible both in men and money.

5. The third effect was an appreciation that in industrial production for military purposes Canada will have to divorce herself from British types and more and more adopt the American. Only in this way can drawings and specifications be counted on, spare parts and tooling be readily available and speed of production increased.

6. The fourth effect has been a growing conviction that as the war comes nearer North America Canada and the United States must concert together so as to be able to prepare effectively to meet an emergency if it should arise. That is why Mackenzie King is pressing for limited staff talks and why he is awaiting the President's answer so anxiously.

7. In short, Canada is at a crossroad. She is about to intensify to the full her war effort and knows that it must be redirected. She is all prepared to direct it along American lines if we give her any encouragement. I hope, therefore, that as a first step we agree to allow naval and air officers of the two countries to make contact and discuss matters freely and informally, and that we may subsequently find other fields where technicians may make contact with a view to synthesizing Canadian defense efforts with our own.

MOFFAT

851.24/187

The British Ambassador (Lothian) to the Secretary of State

No. 315

In a communication which he handed to the Under Secretary of State on November 30, 1939,[22] His Majesty's Ambassador informed the State Department that H. M. Government in the United Kingdom and the French Government had appointed an Anglo-French Purchasing Board in the United States, of which Mr. Arthur B. Purvis would be Chairman and M. Bloch-Lainé, Vice-Chairman.

---

[21] Canadian Prime Minister.
[22] *Foreign Relations*, 1939, vol. I, p. 571.

Lord Lothian has now the honour to inform the State Department that in consequence of the Franco-German armistice,[22a] the Anglo-French Purchasing Board has been dissolved as from July 5th.

The British Purchasing Commission, of which Mr. Purvis is Director-General, will continue with headquarters at 15 Broad Street, New York.

WASHINGTON, July 9, 1940.

841.24/281

The Acting Secretary of State to the British Ambassador (Lothian)

The Acting Secretary of State presents his compliments to His Excellency the British Ambassador and has the honor to acknowledge the receipt of Lord Lothian's note of July 13, 1940,[23] with further reference to the dissolution of the Anglo-French Purchasing Board in the United States.

Lord Lothian may rest assured that this Government will continue to extend to Mr. Arthur B. Purvis, in his new capacity as Director-General of the British Purchasing Commission, the same facilities which were extended to him as Chairman of the Anglo-French Purchasing Board.

WASHINGTON, July 23, 1940.

841.248/634

Memorandum by the Assistant Chief of the Division of Controls (Yost)

[WASHINGTON,] August 26, 1940.

In connection with the purchase of aircraft in this country by the British and Allied Governments, it is interesting to note that during the period June 30 to August 17, inclusive, 1,350 aircraft were ordered and 403 were delivered. Under present contracts it is provided that 89 aircraft will be delivered in the last two weeks of August, 229 in September, 291 in October, 351 in November, 440 in December and increasing numbers in subsequent months mounting to a peak of 846 in August 1941.

CHARLES W. YOST

[22a] For text of the armistice agreement, signed June 22, 1940, see *Documents on German Foreign Policy, 1918–1945*, series D, vol. IX, document No. 523, p. 671.
[23] Not printed.

841.24/340½

The British Prime Minister (Churchill) to President Roosevelt [24]

LONDON, October 27, 1940.

We have not yet heard what Vichy has agreed to.

If, however, they have betrayed warships and African and other Colonial harbours to Hitler, our already heavy task will be grievously aggravated. If Oran and Bizerta become German-Italian submarine bases, our hopes of stopping or impeding the reinforcement of the hostile army now attacking Egypt will be destroyed, and the heaviest form of German-organized Italian attack must be expected. The situation in the Western Mediterranean will also be gravely worsened. If Dakar is betrayed, very great dangers will arise in the Atlantic unless we are able to rectify the position, which will not be easy.

On the other hand, the announcement of Vichy's terms may lead to much desired revolt in the French Empire, which we should have to aid and foster with further drains upon our slowly expanding resources.

Either way, therefore, immense exertions will be required from us in the Mediterranean during the next year.

We are endeavouring to assemble a very large army in the Middle East, and the movement of troops thither from all parts of the Empire, especially from the Mother country, has for some months past been unceasing. The campaign which will develop there certainly in the new year, and which may involve Turkey and Greece, makes demands upon our shipping and munitions output and resources which are enormous and beyond our power without your help to supply to a degree which would ensure victory.

All the time we have to provide for the defence of the island against invasion which is fully mounted and for which sixty of the best German divisions and superior Air Forces stand ready.

Lastly the U-boat and air attacks upon our only remaining life line, the northwestern approach, will be repelled only by the strongest concentration of our flotillas.

You will see, therefore, Mr. President, how very great are our problems and dangers. We feel, however, confident of our ability, if we are given the necessary supplies, to carry on the war to a successful conclusion, and anyhow we are going to try our best.

You will, however, allow me to impress upon you the extreme urgency of accelerating delivery of the programme of aircraft and

---

[24] This message was sent by Sir Arthur Salter, Parliamentary Secretary, British Ministry of Supply, to Arthur B. Purvis, Director-General, British Purchasing Commission in the United States, who in turn transmitted it to Secretary of the Treasury Morgenthau with the request that it be conveyed to President Roosevelt.

other munitions which has already been laid before you by Layton [24a] and Purvis. So far as aircraft is concerned, would it be possible to speed up deliveries of existing orders so that the numbers coming to our support next year will be considerably increased? Furthermore can new orders for expanded programme also be placed so promptly that deliveries may come out in the middle of 1941?

The equipment of our armies, both for home defence and overseas, is progressing, but we depend upon American deliveries to complete our existing programme which will certainly be delayed and impeded by the bombing of factories and disturbances of work.

A memorandum on the technical details is being furnished you through the proper channels,[25] and having placed all the facts before you I feel confident that everything humanly possible will be done. The world cause is in your hands.

[Enclosure] [26]

Memorandum by Mr. Harry L. Hopkins, Special Assistant to President Roosevelt

(1) 10 destroyers a month beginning April 1st. Destroyers to be reconditioned in the United States—reconditioning to begin immediately.

(2) The urgent need of more merchant shipping at once. British cannot wait until new ships are built.

(3) 50 PBY planes in addition to the PBY which the British are receiving on their own account; fully equipped with radio, depth charges, bombs, guns and ammunition. Adequate operating spares supplies. Urgent need for crews.

(4) There are 29 engineless Lockheed planes in England. They need 58 Wright 1820 engines at once.

(5) There are 100 Curtiss Tomahawks without propellers in England. 764 fifty caliber and 1000 thirty caliber machine guns required to complete armament. Curtiss Tomahawks already in England.

(6) Consideration to be given immediately to the replacement of fifty caliber guns manufactured by Colt which are unsatisfactory with the same gun which has already been manufactured by our own arsenals.

(7) 20 million rounds of fifty caliber ammunition and as many extra fifty caliber gun barrels as are available urgently needed.

[24a] Sir Walter Thomas Layton, of the Office of Minister of Production, 1940–42.
[25] See the enclosure to this document.
[26] This memorandum attached to the Department's file copy of the message of Prime Minister Churchill to President Roosevelt is presumably the "memorandum on the technical details" referred to in the last paragraph of that message.

(8)   The maximum number of B 17, BS C's or D's in addition to the 20 already agreed upon to be sent to England immediately. Planes should be sent complete ready for immediate operation, including spare parts, bombs and ammunition. Crews urgently needed.

(9)   Transfer to the British 200 North American Harvards or Vultee Valiants trainers in excess of all present deliveries.

(10)   At least 5 additional civilian flying training schools completely equipped.

(11)   Work out plan to ferry bombers to England. This would release nearly 800 British R. A. F. personnel.

(12)   250,000 Enfield rifles and 50,000,000 rounds of ammunition have been sent.

(13)   Give priority to tools for the manufacture of Point 303 rifles for the British. Same applies to 303 ammunition.

(14)   Send 80 trained observers—half from the factories and half from the Army and Navy—to acquaint Britain with the use of our planes.

HARRY HOPKINS

841.24/359

The British Ambassador (Lothian) to the Secretary of State

No. 589

His Majesty's Ambassador presents his compliments to the Secretary of State and has the honour to inform him that a British Air Commission has been established in the United States for the purpose of co-ordinating, in co-operation with the British Purchasing Commission, the purchase of aircraft and aircraft material in this country on behalf of His Majesty's Government. The Commission is under the direction of Sir Henry Self and its present address is 1785, Massachusetts Avenue, Washington, D. C. (telephone Hobart 9000).

WASHINGTON, November 30, 1940.

740.0011 European War/12–740

The British Prime Minister (Churchill) to President Roosevelt [27]

MY DEAR MR. PRESIDENT: As we reach the end of this year I feel that you will expect me to lay before you the prospects for 1941. I do so strongly and confidently because it seems to me that the vast

---

[27] This message was sent as a telegram from London on December 7, 1940, to the British Ambassador in Washington, who was instructed to transmit it to the Department with the request that the message be forwarded by plane to President Roosevelt, who was on a cruise in the Caribbean. On December 20 the British Embassy transmitted to the President at the request of Prime Minister Churchill certain corrections in the message. These corrections appear here in brackets.

majority of American citizens have recorded their conviction that the safety of the United States as well as the future of our two democracies and the kind of civilisation for which they stand are bound up with the survival and independence of the British Commonwealth of Nations. Only thus can those bastions of sea-power, upon which the control of the Atlantic and the Indian Oceans depends, be preserved in faithful and friendly hands. The control of the Pacific by the United States Navy and of the Atlantic by the British Navy is indispensable to the security of the trade routes of both our countries and the surest means to preventing the war from reaching the shores of the United States.

2. There is another aspect. It takes between three and four years to convert the industries of a modern state to war purposes. Saturation point is reached when the maximum industrial effort that can be spared from civilian needs has been applied to war production. Germany certainly reached this point by the end of 1939. We in the British Empire are now only about half-way through the second year. The United States, I should suppose, was by no means so far advanced as we. Moreover, I understand that immense programmes of naval, military and air defence are now on foot in the United States, to complete which certainly two years are needed. It is our British duty in the common interest as also for our own survival to hold the front and grapple with Nazi power until the preparations of the United States are complete. Victory may come before the two years are out; but we have no right to count upon it to the extent of relaxing any effort that is humanly possible. Therefore I submit with very great respect for your good and friendly consideration that there is a solid identity of interest between the British Empire and the United States while these conditions last. It is upon this footing that I venture to address you.

3. The form which this war has taken and seems likely to hold does not enable us to match the immense armies of Germany in any theatre where their main power can be brought to bear. We can however by the use of sea power and air power meet the German armies in the regions where only comparatively small forces can be brought into action. We must do our best to prevent German domination of Europe spreading into Africa and into Southern Asia. We have also to maintain in constant readiness in this Island armies strong enough to make the problem of an overseas invasion insoluble. For these purposes we are forming as fast as possible, as you are already aware, between fifty and sixty divisions. Even if the United States was our ally instead of our friend and indispensable partner we should not ask for a large American expeditionary army. Shipping, not men, is the limiting factor and the power to transport munitions and supplies claims priority over the movement by sea of large numbers of soldiers.

4. The first half of 1940 was a period of disaster for the Allies and for the Empire. The last five months have witnessed a strong and perhaps unexpected recovery by Great Britain; fighting alone but with invaluable aid in munitions and in destroyers placed at our disposal by the great Republic of which you are for the third time chosen Chief.

5. The danger of Great Britain being destroyed by a swift overwhelming blow has for the time being very greatly receded. In its place there is a long, gradually maturing danger, less sudden and less spectacular but equally deadly. This mortal danger is the steady and increasing diminution of sea tonnage. We can endure the shattering of our dwellings and the slaughter of our civilian population by indiscriminate air attacks and we hope to parry these increasingly as our science develops and to repay them upon military objectives in Germany as our Air Force more nearly approaches the strength of the enemy. The decision for 1941 lies upon the seas; unless we can establish our ability to feed this Island, to import munitions of all kinds which we need, unless we can move our armies to the various theatres where Hitler and his confederate Mussolini must be met, and maintain them there and do all this with the assurance of being able to carry it on till the spirit of the continental dictators is broken, we may fall by the way and the time needed by the United States to complete her defensive preparations may not be forthcoming. It is therefore in shipping and in the power to transport across the oceans, particularly the Atlantic Ocean, that in 1941 the crunch of the whole war will be found. If on the other hand we are able to move the necessary tonnage to and fro across the salt water indefinitely, it may well be that the application of superior air power to the German homeland and the rising anger of the German and other Nazi-gripped populations will bring the agony of civilization to a merciful and glorious end. But do not let us underrate the task.

6. Our shipping losses, the figures for which in recent months are appended,[27a] have been on a scale almost comparable to that of the worst years of the last war. In the 5 weeks ending November 3rd the losses reached a total of 420,300 tons. Our estimation of the annual tonnage which ought to be imported in order to maintain our war effort at full strength is 43,000,000 tons; the tonnage entering in September was only at the rate of 37,000,000 tons and in October at 38,000,000 tons. Were the diminution to continue at this rate it would be fatal, unless indeed immensely greater replenishment than anything at present in sight could be achieved in time. Although we are doing all we can to meet this situation by new methods, the difficulty of limiting the losses is obviously much greater than in the last war. We lack the assistance of the French Navy, the Italian Navy and the Japanese

---

[27a] Not printed.

Navy, and above all the United States Navy, which was of such vital help to us during the culminating years. The enemy commands the ports all around the northern and western coast of France. He is increasingly basing his submarines, flying boats and combat planes on these ports and on the islands off the French coast. We lack [*are denied*] the use of ports or territory [*territories*] in [*of*] Eire in which to organise our coastal patrols by air and sea. In fact, we have now only one effective passage [*route*] of entry to the British Isles, namely, the northern approach, against which the enemy is increasingly concentrating, reaching ever farther out by U–boat action and long distance bombing. In addition, there have for some months been merchant ship raiders both in the Atlantic and in the Indian Oceans. And now we have powerful warship raiders to contend with as well. We need ships both to hunt down and to escort. Large as are our resources and preparations we do not possess enough.

7. The next six or seven months bring the relative battleship strength in home waters to a smaller margin than is satisfactory. The *Bismark* and the *Tirpitz* will certainly be in service in January. We have already the *King George V* and hope to have the *Prince of Wales* at the same time. These modern ships are of course far better armoured, especially against air attack, than vessels like the *Rodney* and *Nelson* designed twenty years ago. We have recently had to use the *Rodney* on trans-Atlantic escort and at any time when numbers are so small, a mine or a torpedo may alter decisively the strength of the line of battle. We get relief in June when the *Duke of York* will be ready and will be still better off at the end of 1941 when the *Anson* also will have joined. But these two first class, modern, thirty-five thousand ton, fifteen inch gun German battleships force us to maintain a concentration never previously necessary in this war.

8. We hope that the two Italian *Littorios* will be out of action for a while and anyway they are not so dangerous as if they were manned by the Germans. Perhaps they might be! We are indebted to you for your help about the *Richelieu* and the *Jean Bart* and I daresay that will be all right. But, Mr. President, as no one will see more clearly than you, we have during these months to consider for the first time in this war, a fleet action in which the enemy will have two ships at least as good as our two best and only two modern ones. It will be impossible to reduce our strength in the Mediterranean because of the attitude of Turkey and indeed the whole position in the Eastern basin depends upon our having a strong fleet there. The older un-modernized battleships will have to go for convoy. Thus even in the battleship class we are at full extension.

9. There is a second field of danger: the Vichy Government may either by joining Hitler's new order in Europe or through some

manoeuvre such as forcing us to attack an expedition despatched by sea against free French Colonies, find an excuse for ranging with the Axis Powers the very considerable undamaged naval forces still under its control. If the French Navy were to join the Axis, the control of West Africa would pass immediately into their hands with the gravest consequences to our communication between the northern and southern Atlantic, and also affect Dakar and of course thereafter South America.

10. A third sphere of danger is in the Far East. Here it seems clear that the Japanese are thrusting Southward through Indo China to Saigon and other naval and air bases, thus bringing them within a comparatively short distance of Singapore and the Dutch East Indies. It is reported that the Japanese are preparing five good divisions for possible use as an overseas expeditionary force. We have to-day no forces in the Far East capable of dealing with this situation should it develop.

11. In the face of these dangers, we must try to use the year 1941 to build up such a supply of weapons, particularly aircraft, both by increased output at home in spite of bombardment, and through ocean-borne supplies, as will lay the foundation of victory. In view of the difficulty and magnitude of this task, as outlined by all the facts I have set forth to which many others could be added, I feel entitled, nay bound, to lay before you the various ways in which the United States could give supreme and decisive help to what is, in certain aspects, the common cause.

12. The prime need is to check or limit the loss of tonnage on the Atlantic approaches to our Islands. This may be achieved both by increasing the naval forces which cope with attacks, and by adding to the number of merchant ships on which we depend. For the first purpose there would seem to be the following alternatives:

(1) the reassertion by the United States of the doctrine of the freedom of the seas from illegal and barbarous warfare in accordance with the decisions reached after the late Great War, and as freely accepted and defined by Germany in 1935. From this, the United States ships should be free to trade with countries against which there is not an effective legal blockade.

(2) It would, I suggest, follow that protection should be given to this lawful trading by United States forces i. e. escorting battleships, cruisers, destroyers and air flotillas. Protection would be immediately more effective if you were able to obtain bases in Eire for the duration of the war. I think it is improbable that such protection would provoke a declaration of war by Germany upon the United States though probably sea incidents of a dangerous character would from time to time occur. Hitler has shown himself inclined to avoid the Kaiser's mistake. He does not wish to be drawn into war with the United States until he has gravely undermined the power of Great Britain. His maxim is "one at a time". The policy I have

ventured to outline, or something like it, would constitute a decisive act of constructive non-belligerency by the United States, and more than any other measure would make it certain that British resistance could be effectively prolonged for the desired period and victory gained.

(3) Failing the above, the gift, loan or supply of a large number of American vessels of war, above all destroyers already in the Atlantic, is indispensable to the maintenance of the Atlantic route. Further, could not United States naval forces extend their sea control over the American side of the Atlantic, so as to prevent molestation by enemy vessels of the approaches to the new line of naval and air bases which the United States is establishing in British islands in the Western Hemisphere. The strength of the United States naval forces is such that the assistance in the Atlantic that they could afford us, as described above, would not jeopardise control over the Pacific.

(4) We should also then need the good offices of the United States and the whole influence of its Government continually exerted, to procure for Great Britain the necessary facilities upon the southern and western shores of Eire for our flotillas, and still more important, for our aircraft, working westward into the Atlantic. If it were proclaimed an American interest that the resistance of Great Britain should be prolonged and the Atlantic route kept open for the important armaments now being prepared for Great Britain in North America, the Irish in the United States might be willing to point out to the Government of Eire the dangers which its present policy is creating for the United States itself.

His Majesty's Government would of course take the most effective steps beforehand to protect Ireland if Irish action exposed it to a German attack. It is not possible for us to compel the people of Northern Ireland against their will to leave the United Kingdom and join Southern Ireland. But I do not doubt that if the Government of Eire would show its solidarity with the democracies of the English speaking world at this crisis a Council of Defence of all Ireland could be set up out of which the unity of the island would probably in some form or other emerge after the war.

13. The object of the foregoing measures is to reduce to manageable proportions the present destructive losses at sea. In addition it is indispensable that the merchant tonnage available for supplying Great Britain and for the waging of the war by Great Britain with all vigour, should be substantially increased beyond the one and a quarter million tons per annum which is the utmost we can now build. The convoy system, the detours, the zig-zags, the great distances from which we now have to bring our imports, and the congestion of our western harbours, have reduced by about one third the value of our existing tonnage. To ensure final victory, not less than three million tons of additional merchant shipbuilding capacity will be required. Only the United States can supply this need. Looking to the future it would seem that production on a scale comparable with that of the Hog Island scheme of the last war ought to be faced

for 1942. In the meanwhile, we ask that in 1941 the United States should make available to us every ton of merchant shipping, surplus to its own requirements, which it possesses or controls and should find some means of putting into our "hands" a large proportion of the merchant shipping now under construction for the National Maritime Board.

14. Moreover we look to the industrial energy of the Republic for a reinforcement of our domestic capacity to manufacture combat aircraft. Without that reinforcement reaching us in a substantial measure, we shall not achieve the massive preponderance in the air on which we must rely to loosen and disintegrate the German grip on Europe. The development of the Air Forces of the Empire provides for a total of nearly 7000 combat aircraft in the fighting squadrons by the spring of 1942, backed by about an equal number in the training units. [*We are at present engaged in a programme designed to increase our strength to 7,000 first line aircraft by the spring of 1942.*] [28] But it is abundantly clear that this programme will not suffice to give us the weighty superiority which will force open the doors of victory. In order to achieve such superiority it is plain that we shall need the greatest production of aircraft which United States of America are capable of sending us. It is our anxious hope that in the teeth of continuing bombardment we shall realize the greater part of production which we have planned in this country. But not even with the addition to our squadrons of all the aircraft which under present arrangements, we may derive from the planned output in the United States can we hope to achieve the necessary ascendancy. May I invite you then, Mr. President, to give earnest consideration to an immediate order on joint account for a further 2,000 combat aircraft a month? Of these aircraft I would submit that the highest possible proportion should be heavy bombers, the weapon on which above all others we depend to shatter the foundations of German military power. I am aware of the formidable task that this would impose upon the industrial organisation of the United States. Yet, in our heavy need, we call with confidence to the most resourceful and ingenious technicians in the world. We ask for an unexampled effort believing that it can be made.

15. You have also received information about the needs of our armies. In the munitions sphere, in spite of enemy bombing, we are making steady progress. Without your continued assistance in the supply of machine tools and in the further release from stock of certain articles we could not hope to equip as many as 50 divisions in 1941. I am grateful for the arrangements already practically completed for your aid in the equipment of the army which we have already planned

---

[28] This sentence to be substituted for preceding one.

house of a neighbor catches fire. If you have a hose and connect it with his hydrant, you may help him to save his house. You don't say to your neighbor that your hose cost $15 and that he must pay $15. After the fire is over, the neighbor might return it with thanks, or if it were smashed, ask how many feet of hose you loaned him. You might say 150 feet, and he would say he would replace it. The President said that if we lend munitions and the like to Great Britain and get them back after the war, if they are intact, it is all right. He said that he did not desire to go into the legal question, but that the broad thought was that we would take over not all of the future British orders but whatever would be necessary. We could enter into an agreement with the British that when the war is over we will get repaid in kind some time. This would substitute for the dollar sign a gentleman's obligation to repay in kind.

At the conclusion of the President's remarks a number of questions were posed by the correspondents. One asked if title to the goods intended for the British would under such an arrangement still remain in our name. In reply, the President said that this would take a lawyer to decide. He gave the following illustration: Suppose that you desire to borrow $4000 or $5000 on your home, which is unencumbered. You give a mortgage, and in your mind you still think it is your home but in the strictest legalistic sense the title has passed to the mortgage-holder. The President said that he did not think it made any difference who held the title to the goods.

A correspondent inquired whether the President thought that such a plan in action would take us more into the war than we are now. The President replied in the negative.

Asked if he had in mind turning over American naval vessels under this plan, the President answered in the negative and said that he referred only to merchant vessels. A correspondent inquired if such ships would be delivered under the American flag the President replied that this would not necessarily be the case, and indicated that it was not necessary to send U. S. flag vessels or crews into war zones.

Asked if these plans involved repeal of the Neutrality Act, the President replied in the negative.

Asked if such a plan applied to articles to be delivered in the future, following present contracts, the President answered in the affirmative. He said that the British have sufficient exchange for present orders, but that there might be a problem in their payment for additional orders.

A correspondent inquired if and when the President intended to present such a plan to Congress. The President replied that he intended to present this or a similar plan after the new Congress opens on January 3, but that the details must be worked out both here and in Great Britain.

and for the provision of American-type weapons for an additional 10 divisions in time for the campaign of 1942. But when the tide of dictatorship begins to recede, many countries, trying to regain their freedom, may be asking for arms, and there is no source to which they can look except to the factories of the United States. I must therefore also urge the importance of expanding to the utmost American productive capacity for small arms, artillery and tanks.

16. I am arranging to present you with a complete programme of munitions of all kinds which we seek to obtain from you, the greater part of which is of course already agreed. An important economy of time and effort will be produced if the types selected for the United States Services should, whenever possible, conform to those which have proved their merit under actual conditions of war. In this way reserves of guns and ammunition and of aeroplanes become interchangeable and are by that very fact augmented. This is however a sphere so highly technical that I do not enlarge upon it.

17. Last of all I come to the question of finance. The more rapid and abundant the flow of munitions and ships which you are able to send us, the sooner will our dollar credits be exhausted. They are already as you know very heavily drawn upon by payments we have made to date. Indeed as you know orders already placed or under negotiation, including expenditures settled or pending for creating munitions factories in the United States, many times exceed the total exchange resources remaining at the disposal of Great Britain. The moment approaches when we shall no longer be able to pay cash for shipping and other supplies. While we will do our utmost and shrink from no proper sacrifice to make payments across the exchange, I believe that you will agree that it would be wrong in principle and mutually disadvantageous in effect if, at the height of this struggle, Great Britain were to be divested of all saleable assets so that after victory was won with our blood, civilisation saved and time gained for the United States to be fully armed against all eventualities, we should stand stripped to the bone. Such a course would not be in the moral or economic interests of either of our countries. We here would be unable after the war to purchase the large balance of imports from the United States over and above the volume of our exports which is agreeable to your tariffs and domestic economy. Not only should we in Great Britain suffer cruel privations but widespread unemployment in the United States would follow the curtailment of American exporting power.

18. Moreover I do not believe the Government and people of the United States would find it in accordance with the principles which guide them, to confine the help which they have so generously promised only to such munitions of war and commodities as could be immediately

paid for. You may be assured that we shall prove ourselves ready to suffer and sacrifice to the utmost for the Cause, and that we glory in being its champion. The rest we leave with confidence to you and to your people, being sure that ways and means will be found which future generations on both sides of the Atlantic will approve and admire.

19. If, as I believe, you are convinced, Mr. President, that the defeat of the Nazi and Fascist tyranny is a matter of high consequence to the people of the United States and to the Western Hemisphere, you will regard this letter not as an appeal for aid, but as a statement of the minimum action necessary to the achievement of our common purpose.

I remain,

Yours very sincerely,

WINSTON S. CHURCHILL

———————

841.24/375

The British Chargé (Butler) to the Secretary of State

No. 623   WASHINGTON, December 16, 1940.

SIR: I have the honour to inform you that His Majesty's Government in the United Kingdom have approved new arrangements for dealing with questions relating to the purchase of supplies from North America. There will be in the United States a Committee to be called the British Supply Council in North America, of which the Chairman will be Mr. Arthur B. Purvis, Director General of the British Purchasing Commission, and the Deputy Chairman Mr. Morris Wilson.

2. The British Supply Council, in harmony with His Majesty's Ambassador, will deal with all issues of policy concerning supplies, including representations made to the United States Administration.

3. In London there will be a Supply Committee, of which the Minister of Supply will be Chairman and the First Lord of the Admiralty and the Minister of Aircraft Production will be members. The representatives in the United States of these three supply ministries will be members of the British Supply Council in North America.

I have the honour [etc.]   BUTLER

———————

841.51/1643 : Telegram

The Secretary of State to the Chargé in the United Kingdom (Johnson)

WASHINGTON, December 20, 1940.

3900. Your 4139, December 19.[29] The following is an unofficial summary of what the President is reported to have said informally as background for correspondents on December 17:

———————

[29] Not printed.

The President said that in the present world situation there was absolutely no doubt in the minds of an overwhelming number of Americans that the best defense of the United States is the security of Great Britain in defending itself; and that therefore, quite aside from the historical interest of this nation in the survival of democracy, it was equally important for us to do everything to help the British Empire to help itself. He said that he had read a lot of nonsense during the last few days about the method of financing British purchases. He said that in his memory and historically no major war had been won or lost through the lack of money. He stated that we had been getting stories which went back to that attitude, and he emphasized that it is not merely a question of our doing things in a traditional way and that there are lots of other ways of doing things. He declared that the one thing that is important is additional production facilities in this country, at shipyards, munitions plants and other places, in order to achieve a strong national defense. He said that orders from Great Britain are therefore a great asset for American defense because they create facilities.

The President said that he was talking from the selfish point of view and that production must be encouraged by us, and that there were several ways of encouraging it—not just one, the way a narrow-minded person might assume. The narrow-minded fellow had assumed that the only way was to repeal certain existing statutes like the Neutrality Act and the Johnson Act,[30] and then lend the money to Great Britain to be spent here. Another way of encouraging such production was perhaps a gift, including gifts to Great Britain of ships, planes, guns, ammunition and the like. In this connection, however, he asked the correspondents if they themselves would ask for a gift if they were in the position of Great Britain. He doubted very much that Great Britain would care to have a gift from the United States. He said that there were also other ways to encourage production and that these were being explored. He could speak only in generalities, and these other ways had been in the process of exploration for three or four weeks.

The President said that it was possible for the United States to take over British orders, and because they are essentially the same kind which we use ourselves we could turn them into American orders and then hand them over upon completion to the British. He explained that we could either lease these materials or sell them subject to a mortgage, on the general theory that it still may prove true that the best defense of Great Britain is the best defense of the United States. What he was trying to do was to eliminate the dollar sign. In this connection he gave the following illustration: Suppose the

———————

[30] 48 Stat. 574.

and for the provision of American-type weapons for an additional 10 divisions in time for the campaign of 1942. But when the tide of dictatorship begins to recede, many countries, trying to regain their freedom, may be asking for arms, and there is no source to which they can look except to the factories of the United States. I must therefore also urge the importance of expanding to the utmost American productive capacity for small arms, artillery and tanks.

16. I am arranging to present you with a complete programme of munitions of all kinds which we seek to obtain from you, the greater part of which is of course already agreed. An important economy of time and effort will be produced if the types selected for the United States Services should, whenever possible, conform to those which have proved their merit under actual conditions of war. In this way reserves of guns and ammunition and of aeroplanes become interchangeable and are by that very fact augmented. This is however a sphere so highly technical that I do not enlarge upon it.

17. Last of all I come to the question of finance. The more rapid and abundant the flow of munitions and ships which you are able to send us, the sooner will our dollar credits be exhausted. They are already as you know very heavily drawn upon by payments we have made to date. Indeed as you know orders already placed or under negotiation, including expenditures settled or pending for creating munitions factories in the United States, many times exceed the total exchange resources remaining at the disposal of Great Britain. The moment approaches when we shall no longer be able to pay cash for shipping and other supplies. While we will do our utmost and shrink from no proper sacrifice to make payments across the exchange, I believe that you will agree that it would be wrong in principle and mutually disadvantageous in effect if, at the height of this struggle, Great Britain were to be divested of all saleable assets so that after victory was won with our blood, civilisation saved and time gained for the United States to be fully armed against all eventualities, we should stand stripped to the bone. Such a course would not be in the moral or economic interests of either of our countries. We here would be unable after the war to purchase the large balance of imports from the United States over and above the volume of our exports which is agreeable to your tariffs and domestic economy. Not only should we in Great Britain suffer cruel privations but widespread unemployment in the United States would follow the curtailment of American exporting power.

18. Moreover I do not believe the Government and people of the United States would find it in accordance with the principles which guide them, to confine the help which they have so generously promised only to such munitions of war and commodities as could be immediately

paid for. You may be assured that we shall prove ourselves ready to suffer and sacrifice to the utmost for the Cause, and that we glory in being its champion. The rest we leave with confidence to you and to your people, being sure that ways and means will be found which future generations on both sides of the Atlantic will approve and admire.

19. If, as I believe, you are convinced, Mr. President, that the defeat of the Nazi and Fascist tyranny is a matter of high consequence to the people of the United States and to the Western Hemisphere, you will regard this letter not as an appeal for aid, but as a statement of the minimum action necessary to the achievement of our common purpose.

I remain,

Yours very sincerely,

WINSTON S. CHURCHILL

841.24/375

The British Chargé (Butler) to the Secretary of State

No. 623   WASHINGTON, December 16, 1940.

SIR: I have the honour to inform you that His Majesty's Government in the United Kingdom have approved new arrangements for dealing with questions relating to the purchase of supplies from North America. There will be in the United States a Committee to be called the British Supply Council in North America, of which the Chairman will be Mr. Arthur B. Purvis, Director General of the British Purchasing Commission, and the Deputy Chairman Mr. Morris Wilson.

2. The British Supply Council, in harmony with His Majesty's Ambassador, will deal with all issues of policy concerning supplies, including representations made to the United States Administration.

3. In London there will be a Supply Committee, of which the Minister of Supply will be Chairman and the First Lord of the Admiralty and the Minister of Aircraft Production will be members. The representatives in the United States of these three supply ministries will be members of the British Supply Council in North America.

I have the honour [etc.]   BUTLER

841.51/1643 : Telegram

*The Secretary of State to the Chargé in the United Kingdom
(Johnson)*

WASHINGTON, December 20, 1940.

3900. Your 4139, December 19.[29] The following is an unofficial summary of what the President is reported to have said informally as background for correspondents on December 17:

---

[29] Not printed.

The President said that in the present world situation there was absolutely no doubt in the minds of an overwhelming number of Americans that the best defense of the United States is the security of Great Britain in defending itself; and that therefore, quite aside from the historical interest of this nation in the survival of democracy, it was equally important for us to do everything to help the British Empire to help itself. He said that he had read a lot of nonsense during the last few days about the method of financing British purchases. He said that in his memory and historically no major war had been won or lost through the lack of money. He stated that we had been getting stories which went back to that attitude, and he emphasized that it is not merely a question of our doing things in a traditional way and that there are lots of other ways of doing things. He declared that the one thing that is important is additional production facilities in this country, at shipyards, munitions plants and other places, in order to achieve a strong national defense. He said that orders from Great Britain are therefore a great asset for American defense because they create facilities.

The President said that he was talking from the selfish point of view and that production must be encouraged by us, and that there were several ways of encouraging it—not just one, the way a narrow-minded person might assume. The narrow-minded fellow had assumed that the only way was to repeal certain existing statutes like the Neutrality Act and the Johnson Act,[30] and then lend the money to Great Britain to be spent here. Another way of encouraging such production was perhaps a gift, including gifts to Great Britain of ships, planes, guns, ammunition and the like. In this connection, however, he asked the correspondents if they themselves would ask for a gift if they were in the position of Great Britain. He doubted very much that Great Britain would care to have a gift from the United States. He said that there were also other ways to encourage production and that these were being explored. He could speak only in generalities, and these other ways had been in the process of exploration for three or four weeks.

The President said that it was possible for the United States to take over British orders, and because they are essentially the same kind which we use ourselves we could turn them into American orders and then hand them over upon completion to the British. He explained that we could either lease these materials or sell them subject to a mortgage, on the general theory that it still may prove true that the best defense of Great Britain is the best defense of the United States. What he was trying to do was to eliminate the dollar sign. In this connection he gave the following illustration: Suppose the

[30] 48 Stat. 574.

house of a neighbor catches fire. If you have a hose and connect it with his hydrant, you may help him to save his house. You don't say to your neighbor that your hose cost $15 and that he must pay $15. After the fire is over, the neighbor might return it with thanks, or if it were smashed, ask how many feet of hose you loaned him. You might say 150 feet, and he would say he would replace it. The President said that if we lend munitions and the like to Great Britain and get them back after the war, if they are intact, it is all right. He said that he did not desire to go into the legal question, but that the broad thought was that we would take over not all of the future British orders but whatever would be necessary. We could enter into an agreement with the British that when the war is over we will get repaid in kind some time. This would substitute for the dollar sign a gentleman's obligation to repay in kind.

At the conclusion of the President's remarks a number of questions were posed by the correspondents. One asked if title to the goods intended for the British would under such an arrangement still remain in our name. In reply, the President said that this would take a lawyer to decide. He gave the following illustration: Suppose that you desire to borrow $4000 or $5000 on your home, which is unencumbered. You give a mortgage, and in your mind you still think it is your home but in the strictest legalistic sense the title has passed to the mortgage-holder. The President said that he did not think it made any difference who held the title to the goods.

A correspondent inquired whether the President thought that such a plan in action would take us more into the war than we are now. The President replied in the negative.

Asked if he had in mind turning over American naval vessels under this plan, the President answered in the negative and said that he referred only to merchant vessels. A correspondent inquired if such ships would be delivered under the American flag the President replied that this would not necessarily be the case, and indicated that it was not necessary to send U. S. flag vessels or crews into war zones.

Asked if these plans involved repeal of the Neutrality Act, the President replied in the negative.

Asked if such a plan applied to articles to be delivered in the future, following present contracts, the President answered in the affirmative. He said that the British have sufficient exchange for present orders, but that there might be a problem in their payment for additional orders.

A correspondent inquired if and when the President intended to present such a plan to Congress. The President replied that he intended to present this or a similar plan after the new Congress opens on January 3, but that the details must be worked out both here and in Great Britain.